Y0-AWJ-059

WITHDRAWN

915.1   Lye, Keith
Lye
        Take a trip to Hong Kong

	DATE DUE		

SE POLK DELAWARE
ELEMENTARY LIBRARY

SE POLK DELAWARE
ELEMENTARY LIBRARY

Take a trip to
HONG KONG

Keith Lye
General Editor
Henry Pluckrose

Franklin Watts
London   New York   Sydney   Toronto

Facts about Hong Kong

Area:
1,045 sq. km. (403 sq. miles).

Population:
5,021,000 (1981)

Capital:
Victoria (pop. 767,000)

Other cities:
Kowloon, Tsuen Wan

Official languages:
English, Chinese

Main religions:
Buddhism, Taoism, Confucianism, Christianity

Major exports:
Clothing and textile fabrics, watches and clocks, toys and dolls

Currency: Dollar

Franklin Watts Limited
12a Golden Square
London W1

ISBN: UK Edition 0 86313 071 2
ISBN: US Edition 0 531 04740 7

© Franklin Watts Limited 1983

Typeset by Ace Filmsetting Ltd, Frome, Somerset
Printed in Hong Kong

Text Editor: Brenda Williams
Maps: Tony Payne
Design: Mushroom Production
Stamps: Stanley Gibbons Limited
Photographs: Zefa; Colorpix/Ron Carter, 6, 18, 26, 31; Hong Kong Tourist Association, 17, 24, 27, 28; James Davis, 3, 11, 19; Keystone Press, 12
Front Cover: Zefa
Back Cover: J. Allan Cash

The British colony of Hong Kong is a small territory on the coast of southern China. Its capital is Victoria, which stands on Hong Kong island. Hong Kong itself includes 235 other islands and an area on the mainland of China. The mainland city of Kowloon can be seen in the distance.

Ferry boats link Hong Kong's many islands. This picture was taken on Kowloon's waterfront. It shows Victoria and Victoria Peak, a mountain on Hong Kong island.

English signs in this Kowloon street show that westerners have left their mark on Hong Kong. But Chinese traditions are still strong.

5

This old couple wear traditional clothes. In Hong Kong, 98 people out of every 100 are Chinese. More than half of them were born in Hong Kong. But many are refugees from China.

Farming is not an important industry in Hong Kong. Rice is grown in flooded fields, and every piece of land that can be farmed is used. But only three out of every 100 people work on farms. So Hong Kong buys food from abroad.

This picture shows some stamps and money used in Hong Kong. The main unit of currency is the dollar, which is divided into 100 cents.

8

Hong Kong

CHINA
Sheung Shui
Yuen Long
Tai Po
Tuen Mun
NEW TERRITORIES
Tsuen Wan
Shah Tin
Kowloon
Stonecutter Is.
Victoria
Lantau Is.
Hong Kong Is
Aberdeen
Cheung Chau Is.
Lamma Is.
SOUTH CHINA SEA

This busy street is in Victoria. Hong Kong is one of the world's most crowded countries. Nine out of every ten of its people live in cities and towns.

Western clothes are worn in the business district of Victoria. Trading is important in Hong Kong. It is a free port, which means that the government does not charge money on goods from abroad. So goods from all over the world are stored and resold in Hong Kong.

Hong Kong island became a British colony in 1841. Kowloon and Stonecutter Island were added in 1860. In 1898 China leased to Britain many other islands and a mainland area which together are called the New Territories. The lease ends in 1997. Here Queen Elizabeth arrives on a visit.

These men are being trained to serve in the Royal Hong Kong Police Force. Some police officers work on ocean-going launches or jet boats, which patrol Hong Kong's many waterways.

Many electronic goods are made in Hong Kong. They include clocks and watches, radios and television sets. This small territory is the world's leading producer of radios. Over half of the country's working people have jobs in manufacturing industries.

Beautiful fabrics are on sale in Hong Kong. Clothing and textile materials are the country's most valuable exports.

Hong Kong has many open-air markets, where people buy fresh food and other goods. Hong Kong depends on China for much of its food. It even has to buy extra fresh water from China.

Visitors to Hong Kong enjoy the many varied dishes cooked in its Chinese restaurants. Some tourists learn how to eat with chopsticks, like those used by the cook in this picture.

Aberdeen is on the southern side of Hong Kong island and was once a haunt of Chinese pirates. Its sheltered waters are now used by large floating restaurants, where fresh seafood is always on the menu.

Hong Kong is famous for four main kinds of Chinese cooking. Cantonese dishes are the most popular. They are less spicy than Pekingese and Szechuan food, while Shanghai dishes are sweeter and oilier than the others.

More than 2.5 million tourists visit Hong Kong every year. Among its many attractions are the Tiger Balm Gardens, which are often called a Chinese "Disneyland". Statues in the gardens show stories from Chinese legends.

Repulse Bay is a popular beach on the south coast of Hong Kong island. Hong Kong has dry, sunny winters and hot summers. In summer, hurricane storms called typhoons sometimes reach the islands from the ocean.

Housing is in short supply in crowded Hong Kong. Small boats called junks and sampans are homes for thousands of fishermen and their families.

More and more buildings go up in Hong Kong. Many people now live in large apartment blocks, like these in Kowloon.

Children in Hong Kong must spend six years at a primary school and three years at a junior secondary school. Education at these schools is free. Children are taught in both Chinese and English.

These children are visiting Lantau, the largest of Hong Kong's 236 islands. It was once a hideout for pirates. People now visit Lantau for its fine beaches or to see its Buddhist temples and Buddhist and Christian monasteries.

The chief religions in Hong Kong are Buddhism, Taoism and Confucianism. There are also some Christians and Muslims. The Temple of the 10,000 Buddhas is in Shatin valley in the New Territories. Its altar room has over 12,000 statues of the Buddha.

Women wear their best clothes at a family wedding. Parents once decided who their children would marry. People can now choose their own wives or husbands. But most couples still ask their parents to agree to their choice.

Puppet plays have been popular in China since ancient times. These rod puppets are fixed to long sticks. Shorter sticks are used to make the hands move. Music from Cantonese opera is often sung during a play's performance.

Hong Kong has 17 public holidays a year. This child is dressed for the Taoist festival held on the island of Cheung Chau in May. During the festival, towers of buns are built outside the Pak Tai temple.

Boat races are held at the Dragon Boat Festival. This event recalls the tale of a poet who threw himself into a river rather than live under an evil government. The story is over two thousand years old.

The border with China reminds us that China may ask Britain to return the New Territories in 1997 when the lease runs out. Today, China and Hong Kong are on friendly terms. Many people from Hong Kong visit China to see their relatives.

Index

Aberdeen 18

Buddhism 25, 26

Cheung Chau 29
China 3, 6, 12, 16, 31
Chopsticks 17
Climate 21
Clothing 6, 11, 15
Cooking 19

Dragon Boat Festival 30

Education 24
Electronic products 14
Exports 15

Farming 7
Ferry boats 4
Food 16–19

Government 12

History 12
Housing 22–23

Junks 22

Kowloon 3–5, 12, 23

Marriage 27
Money 8

New Territories 12, 26, 31

People 6
Police 13
Public holidays 29
Puppets 28

Religion 26
Repulse Bay 21
Rice fields 7

Sampans 22
Schools 24
Stamps 8

Taoism 26, 29
Temple of 10,000
    Buddhas 26
Textiles 15
Tiger Balm Gardens 20
Tourism 20
Trade 11
Typhoons 21

Victoria 3, 4, 10, 11